Light in the Darkness Overcoming Depression with God's Help

Brygitt A. Ramirez

Table of Contents

Acknowledgments 4
Introduction 6
Connect with me on social media 8
Chapter 1 10
    Understanding Depression.
Chapter 2 16
    The Causes of Depression: Spiritual and Physical.
Chapter 3 24
    Hope in God Amidst Depression.
Chapter 4 32
    Breaking the Chains of Depression.
Chapter 5 40
    The Power of Praise and Worship.
Chapter 6 48
    Restoring Life's Purpose with God.
Chapter 7 56
    The Importance of the Christian Community.
Chapter 8 66
    Prayer and Spiritual Counseling to Overcome Depression.
Chapter 9 76
    Maintaining Peace and Joy in God.

Chapter 10... 86
> Testimonies and Conclusion: Walking in Faith Toward the Future.

Conclusion..100

Acknowledgments

Writing this book has been a deeply personal and transformative experience. Like many, I have witnessed the pain of depression up close, and I know how difficult it can be to face it, both from within and from the outside. This book is not merely the result of research or a collection of thoughts on faith, but a sincere response to the struggles that many of us face in silence.

During the process of creation, I realized something that I already knew but needed to be reminded of: God is with us at every moment of our lives, especially in the darkest times. Although in the midst of pain it may seem as if His presence has faded, His light never stops shining, and His hand is always extended towards us, waiting for us to return to Him.

This book was born from an idea by my husband, Pastor David Rodriguez, and my desire to share a message of hope, to remind whoever reads it that no matter how deep the darkness, there is always a way out.

Depression does not have the final word; God does, and His word is life, peace, and restoration.

I want to dedicate these pages to every person who has felt the weight of despair and to those who seek answers in the midst of their struggles. My prayer is that you find in these words a source of strength and, above all, a guide to draw closer to God, who is our refuge and salvation.

Throughout my life, I have witnessed God's healing grace, both in myself and in those around me. This book is a reflection of that grace, and I hope it touches your heart in the same way it has touched mine while writing it.

Thank you for allowing me to be a part of your journey. May the Lord light your path, and may you find in Him the peace you so deeply long for.

With gratitude,

Copyright, Brygitt Ramirez 2024

Introduction

Depression is a painful reality that affects millions of people, regardless of age, all around the world. For those who experience it, it often feels like a prison of hopelessness, where the light of peace and joy is difficult to reach. However, in the midst of this dark outlook, there is a real and powerful hope: the help of God. Throughout the pages of this book, you will discover that you are not alone in your struggle and that the God who created you has a plan to free and restore you.

This book has been written with the purpose of guiding you toward that hope, showing how the Word of God, prayer, praise, and the Christian community can be powerful tools to break the chains of depression. Step by step, we will explore the causes of depression from both a spiritual and physical perspective, but more importantly, we will see how God can heal even the deepest wounds and give us a renewed purpose for our lives.

This is not just a book of advice or practical strategies. It is an invitation to walk with God in your healing process, to trust in His promise that, in the midst of trials, He is with you and has a future filled with hope and purpose for you. Here, you will find several testimonies of people who, like you, have struggled with depression and have found freedom in Christ. Through their stories, you will discover that restoration is possible and that God is always at work, even when we cannot see it.

As you explore each chapter, I encourage you to do so with an open heart, seeking God's guidance in your life. Remember, this is a journey, and like any healing process, it will require time, patience, and faith. No matter how deep your struggle may be, God is greater. He is faithful to walk with you, to sustain you, and ultimately, to lead you into a life of peace and joy in His presence.

May the words in this book serve as a spiritual guide, but more than that, may they draw you closer to the God who loves you infinitely and who longs to set you free. Depression does not have the final word; God does, and His word for you is life, freedom, and restoration.

Connect with me on social media

I invite you to be part of a community where we share reflections, inspiration, and words of encouragement based on faith. Follow me on my social media platforms so we can continue this journey together, where you'll find messages that strengthen the spirit and bring us closer to God. I look forward to welcoming you with open arms as we keep growing in the light of His love!

Chapter 1

Understanding Depression

What is Depression?

Depression goes beyond just having a bad day or feeling sad. It is a prolonged state of hopelessness, emptiness, and sorrow. Often, those who suffer from it feel that life has lost its meaning, experience constant fatigue, lose interest in activities they once enjoyed, have trouble concentrating, and in extreme cases, may have thoughts of self-harm or suicide.

The modern world offers many explanations for depression: from chemical imbalances in the brain to the stress of social media, isolation, or academic and social pressures. However, from a Christian perspective, we must also consider the spiritual impact. The enemy, Satan, uses every possible means to steal our peace and keep us trapped in despair. Yet in Christ, we find the truth that sets us free.

"The Lord is close to the brokenhearted and saves those who are crushed in spirit." – Psalm 34:18

This verse reminds us that God is not indifferent to our suffering. He sees our tears, hears our prayers, and draws near when our hearts are broken. His presence is our refuge in the midst of pain.

Signs and Symptoms of Depression

It is crucial to learn how to recognize the signs of depression, both in ourselves and in those around us. Some of the most common symptoms include:

- Persistent feelings of sadness or emptiness.
- Loss of interest in activities that once brought joy.
- Changes in sleep patterns (insomnia or excessive sleep).
- Fatigue and lack of energy, even after rest.
- Feelings of worthlessness, guilt, or hopelessness.
- Thoughts of death or suicide.

If you recognize these symptoms in yourself or know someone who is experiencing them, you should not ignore them. Acknowledging depression is the first step toward seeking help and healing, both emotionally and spiritually.

A Christian Perspective on Depression

Depression can often lead us to feel distant from God. We may ask, "Where are You, Lord? Why are You allowing me to feel this way?" These feelings are valid and understandable, but the truth is that God never abandons us. Even when we don't fully understand the purpose of suffering, we can trust that He has a greater plan.

"The thief comes only to steal and kill and destroy; I have come that they may have life, and have it to the full." – John 10:10

Jesus warns us that the enemy tries to steal our joy, destroy our hopes, and keep us trapped in despair. But He also assures us that He came to give us abundant life, a life filled with peace, purpose, and hope. Even when we walk through the valley of the shadow of death, we can hold on to the promise that we are not alone.

God Understands Our Suffering

At times, depression can make us feel like no one understands what we are going through. But in moments of darkness, it's essential to remember that Jesus, the Son of God, experienced pain, anguish, and sorrow. In the Garden of Gethsemane, just before His arrest, Jesus prayed in such agony that His sweat became like drops of blood *(Luke 22:44)*. He understands what it is to feel overwhelmed and afflicted.

God not only understands our suffering but is willing to walk with us through it. In moments of despair, we must remember that He is our strength and refuge.

Key Verse for This Chapter

Psalm 34:18 offers us comfort and assures us that God is close to the brokenhearted. This is a reminder that, even when we feel alone or trapped in darkness, God is nearer than we think. We can turn to Him in prayer, trusting that His love is great enough to lift us out of the depths of depression.

This chapter lays a solid foundation for understanding depression from a Christian perspective, acknowledging the seriousness of the condition and emphasizing that, with God's help, there is always hope.

Before concluding this chapter, I encourage you to say this prayer:

Lord, today I come before You acknowledging my pain and confusion. Sometimes depression overwhelms me, and I don't know how to move forward. I ask that You help me understand what I'm feeling and guide me through this difficult time. Thank You because You are close to the brokenhearted. Give me the strength to seek You in the midst of my sadness and to trust that You have a purpose for me, even when I cannot see it. Amen.

Chapter 2

The Causes of Depression: Spiritual and Physical

Depression, like many other emotional struggles, can be triggered by various causes. Some factors are clearly visible and recognized by society, such as changes in life circumstances, stress, or hormonal imbalances. However, from a Christian perspective, it is also important to recognize that depression has a spiritual dimension. In this chapter, we will explore both the physical and spiritual causes of depression and how the enemy uses these situations to distort our perception of life and of God.

Common factors that trigger depression

Depression is often linked to a combination of factors. Some of them are external, while others are internal, but all can contribute to an overwhelming sense of hopelessness.

- **Broken or toxic relationships**: Family problems, damaging friendships, or romantic relationships that fail can leave deep emotional scars. Rejection, betrayal, or emotional abuse can severely affect self-esteem and mental health.
- **Academic and social pressure**: Many feel overwhelmed by the expectations of success, whether in school, college, or social relationships. Constant comparison on social media and the pressure to meet certain standards can generate feelings of inadequacy.
- **Loneliness and misunderstanding**: Despite living in a highly connected world, many, especially young people, feel alone in their struggles. The lack of a strong support system, such as family or church, can lead them to believe that no one understands what they are experiencing.
- **Physical and hormonal imbalances**: Biological changes, such as those associated with adolescence and growth, can contribute to emotional imbalances. In addition, certain physical health issues, such as vitamin deficiencies or sleep disorders, can exacerbate symptoms of depression.

The impact of drifting away from God

In the spiritual realm, drifting away from God can be a significant factor in depression. When we distance ourselves from our Creator, it is easy to lose sight of our purpose and fall into hopelessness. Satan, known as the accuser, constantly seeks to drive us away from the light of God. One of his most powerful tools is discouragement, and depression is one of the methods he uses to convince us that we are alone, directionless, and without worth.

"The thief comes only to steal and kill and destroy; I have come that they may have life, and have it to the full." – John 10:10

This verse highlights the contrast between the enemy's intentions and Christ's. Satan wants to destroy our peace and steal our joy. However, Jesus came to give us a full life, filled with purpose, joy, and satisfaction in God. Drifting away from God—whether through disobedience, lack of faith, or distractions with worldly things—can open the door to despair.

Losing connection with God is not always evident. Sometimes it is a gradual process. Daily stress, life's distractions, and external influences can slowly separate us from prayer, reading the Word, and fellowship with other believers. As we distance ourselves from these spiritual pillars, the enemy seizes the opportunity to sow doubt, fear, and hopelessness in our minds.

Recognizing the spiritual root

It is important to discern when depression has a spiritual root. While medical science can offer valuable diagnoses and treatments for the physical causes of depression, we must not ignore the spiritual battle that may be occurring. The enemy attacks our mind and heart, seeking to lead us into darkness.

"For our struggle is not against flesh and blood, but against the rulers, against the authorities, against the powers of this dark world..." – Ephesians 6:12

This verse reminds us that many of the struggles we face, including depression, are not merely physical or emotional but are connected to a larger spiritual battle. Satan wants to convince us that there is no hope, that we are alone, and that we will never climb out of the pit of despair. However, God equips us with the spiritual tools necessary to resist these attacks.

How God can use adversity for our good

While depression is a painful experience, the Word of God assures us that in His sovereignty, He can use even the most difficult situations for our good. Sometimes, moments of darkness can draw us closer to God, making us more dependent on His grace and power. Through brokenness, we can find a deeper relationship with Him and experience His restoration.

"And we know that in all things God works for the good of those who love Him, who have been called according to His purpose." – Romans 8:28

This verse is a promise that God does not waste our pain. Even when we don't understand why we are going through a season of depression, we can trust that God is working in us and through us, to mold us and make us more like Christ.

Balancing the physical and spiritual

To overcome depression, it is important to recognize both the physical and spiritual causes. Physical self-care is vital: healthy eating, exercise, and adequate rest can make a significant difference in our emotional state. But we must not neglect spiritual care. Spending time in God's Word, prayer, and surrounding ourselves with a loving and supportive Christian community are essential for our healing.

God created us as complete beings—with body, mind, and spirit—and to heal fully, we must address all these aspects in a balanced way.

Key Verse for This Chapter

John 10:10 reminds us of the battle we face against the enemy and the promise of abundant life in Christ. Satan seeks to destroy us, but Jesus came to give us life and hope. As we advance in understanding the causes of depression, it is crucial to hold on to the truth that in Jesus, there is victory, even over the deepest sorrow.

Before concluding this chapter, I encourage you to say this prayer:

Heavenly Father, I know that depression can have many roots, both physical and spiritual. Today, I ask You to give me discernment to understand the causes of my struggle. Help me to identify the lies of the enemy and to renew my mind with Your truth. May I see my life from Your perspective and trust that You can restore every part of my being. I ask for healing, both for my body and my spirit. In the name of Jesus, Amen.

Chapter 3

Hope in God Amidst Depression

In the midst of depression, it's easy to feel like hope has vanished. Days seem endless, and nights are filled with restlessness and anguish. However, for those who trust in God, there is always a light at the end of the tunnel. The Word of God is filled with promises that remind us He never abandons us, even in our darkest moments. In this chapter, we will explore how we can find hope in God, even when depression feels overwhelming, and how that hope can sustain and lift us.

The Power of Prayer in Dark Times

Prayer is one of the most powerful tools God has given us to face our struggles. When we feel powerless, when we lack the words to express our pain, God invites us to cry out to Him. No matter how deep our wounds are or how great our despair, God is always ready to listen and respond.

"Call to me and I will answer you and tell you great and unsearchable things you do not know." — Jeremiah 33:3

God promises that when we call upon Him, He answers us. Sometimes, the answer doesn't come immediately or in the way we expect, but we can trust that God is working in our lives. Prayer is not only a way to express our needs but also a reminder of who God is—our loving Father who never leaves or forsakes us.

In the darkest moments of depression, we need to draw closer to God in prayer. Even if our words are few or filled with tears, God hears them. When we don't know what to say, the Holy Spirit intercedes for us.

"In the same way, the Spirit helps us in our weakness. We do not know what we ought to pray for, but the Spirit himself intercedes for us through wordless groans." — Romans 8:26

This verse offers great comfort. When we are overwhelmed and can't find the right words to pray, the Holy Spirit helps, carrying our prayers to God. He understands what we're going through, even when we can't express it.

Scriptures of Comfort and Hope

The Bible is filled with verses that remind us that, even though our circumstances may be difficult, God is with us and offers hope. Here are some key passages we can meditate on and pray when depression overwhelms us:

"The righteous cry out, and the Lord hears them; he delivers them from all their troubles. The Lord is close to the brokenhearted and saves those who are crushed in spirit." — Psalm 34:17-18

This passage is a clear promise that God is near us when we are suffering. He not only hears us but also delivers us from our troubles. He may not do so in the way or timing we expect, but we can trust that He is working on our behalf.

"But those who hope in the Lord will renew their strength. They will soar on wings like eagles; they will run and not grow weary, they will walk and not be faint." — Isaiah 40:31

This verse reminds us that hope in God renews our strength. Depression can make us feel exhausted and drained, but God promises to give us the strength to move forward. By trusting in Him, we can find the energy we need to face each day.

The Comfort of the Holy Spirit in Our Pain

One of the greatest comforts for believers is knowing that we are not alone in our moments of sadness. Jesus promised to send the Holy Spirit, our Comforter, to be with us and guide us. In times of depression, the Holy Spirit is there to remind us of God's promises and to give us peace.

"And I will ask the Father, and he will give you another advocate to help you and be with you forever—the Spirit of truth. The world cannot accept him, because it neither sees him nor knows him. But you know him, for he lives with you and will be in you." — John 14:16-17

The Holy Spirit is not only with us but dwells within us. He comforts us when the pain feels unbearable and reminds us that God is with us and that we are not alone in this struggle.

Hope in the Resurrection and the Future God Promises

One of the great promises of Christianity is the hope of resurrection and eternal life. Although depression can make us feel that this life is full of suffering, God assures us that there is a glorious future awaiting those who trust in Him. Hope in eternity can anchor our souls, reminding us that the pain of this world is temporary and that in Christ, we have the promise of eternal peace and joy.

"For to me, to live is Christ and to die is gain."
— Philippians 1:21

The apostle Paul understood that, regardless of the circumstances of this life, his hope was in Christ. Living for Christ brings purpose and meaning, even in the midst of pain. And for believers, death is not the end but the beginning of eternal life in the presence of God.

"He will wipe every tear from their eyes. There will be no more death or mourning or crying or pain, for the old order of things has passed away." — Revelation 21:4

This verse in Revelation reminds us that one day, all suffering will cease. No more tears, no more pain. God promises us a new life, free from everything that causes sadness and despair. This is the ultimate hope we have in Christ—eternal life of joy in His presence.

Keeping Hope Alive in Difficult Times

Hope is something we must nurture constantly. When we face depression, it's easy to lose sight of God's promises. That's why it's vital to surround ourselves with reminders of His faithfulness. Here are some ways to keep hope alive:

- **Meditate on God's Word daily**: Spend time each day reading and reflecting on God's promises. Verses like *Psalm 23* or *Isaiah 41:10* are great reminders that God is with us.
- **Surround yourself with a Christian community**: Seek people in your church or circle of friends who can support you through prayer and encouragement. We should not face depression alone; God has given us a spiritual family to help us.
- **Praise God despite the circumstances**: Praise is a powerful way to

overcome discouragement. Even when you don't feel joy, praise God for His faithfulness and love. Praise has the power to change the spiritual atmosphere and bring peace to our hearts.

Key Verse for This Chapter

Isaiah 41:10 offers a powerful promise that God is with us, strengthening and helping us in the midst of our struggles:

"So do not fear, for I am with you; do not be dismayed, for I am your God. I will strengthen you and help you; I will uphold you with my righteous right hand."

God is not only with us but promises to help, strengthen, and sustain us. In the midst of depression, we can hold on to this promise with the certainty that God will not let us fall.

Before concluding this chapter, I encourage you to say this prayer:

Lord Jesus, in the midst of my depression, I cling to the hope I have in You. I know that even though my heart is weighed down, Your love never fails. Fill my life with Your peace and comfort me when I feel lost. Help me find strength in Your Word and remember that, in You, there is always hope. Don't let my pain drive me away from You, but use it to draw me closer to Your heart. Amen.

Chapter 4

Breaking the Chains of Depression

Depression is like an invisible prison that locks the mind and heart, preventing us from seeing the light of hope and God's purpose. Many people feel that, once they fall into the darkness of depression, it's impossible to escape. However, God's Word teaches us that in Christ, there is power to break any chain that binds us. This chapter focuses on how, with God's help, we can break the chains of depression and walk in the freedom He has promised us.

Understanding the Enemy's Lies

One of the most effective ways the enemy works to keep us trapped in depression is through lies. Satan is the "father of lies" (*John 8:44*), and he constantly bombards us with thoughts of hopelessness, worthlessness, and failure. These negative thoughts do not come from God, and it's essential that we identify them in order to combat them with truth.

Some of the most common lies the enemy uses include:

- **"You will never get out of this"**: The enemy wants us to believe that depression is a life sentence, something we can never be free from. However, God promises us freedom. Jesus said, "You will know the truth, and the truth will set you free." (*John 8:32*)
- **"You are worthless"**: The devil tries to erode our self-esteem and convince us that we have no value. But God's truth says otherwise: we are His creation, made in His image and likeness (Genesis 1:27). In Christ, we are loved, accepted, and valued.
- **"God has forgotten you"**: In times of suffering, the enemy sows doubt about God's love and faithfulness. But the Bible assures us that God never abandons us. "Though my father and mother forsake me, the Lord will receive me." (*Psalm 27:10*).

Identifying these lies is the first step in breaking the chains of depression. By confronting them with the truth of God's Word, we can begin to see the light in the midst of darkness.

The Importance of Renewing the Mind

Renewing our mind is essential for breaking free from the patterns of thought that fuel depression. The Bible urges us not to conform to this world, but to be transformed by the renewal of our minds:

"Do not conform to the pattern of this world, but be transformed by the renewing of your mind. Then you will be able to test and approve what God's will is—His good, pleasing and perfect will." — *Romans 12:2*

Renewing the mind involves changing the way we think, discarding negative and destructive thoughts, and replacing them with God's truth. This is not something that happens overnight, but a daily process that requires discipline in feeding our minds with God's Word. Meditating on Scripture, praying, and focusing on what is true, honorable, just, and pure (*Philippians 4:8*) are key steps to renewing the mind and fighting depression.

The Power of Confession and Prayer

Confession has tremendous power in the healing process. Sometimes, depression can be linked to unconfessed sins, past guilt, or emotional wounds that we haven't fully surrendered to God. The Bible encourages us to confess our faults to receive healing:

"Therefore confess your sins to each other and pray for each other so that you may be healed. The prayer of a righteous person is powerful and effective." — James 5:16

Opening our hearts to God in prayer and being honest with Him about our struggles is fundamental to breaking the chains of depression. Through confession, we can release the weight of guilt, shame, and pain we've been carrying. It's also important to seek the prayers of other believers who can support and strengthen us spiritually.

Testimonies of Freedom

The Bible is full of examples of people who, like us, experienced moments of despair and depression but found freedom in God. One of the most powerful examples is King David.

Despite being known as a "man after God's own heart," David went through deep sorrow, as expressed in many of the Psalms. However, he always turned back to God, acknowledging His power to deliver.

"I waited patiently for the Lord; he turned to me and heard my cry. He lifted me out of the slimy pit, out of the mud and mire; he set my feet on a rock and gave me a firm place to stand." — Psalm 40:1-2

God delivered David from the "pit of despair," and in the same way, He can deliver us. The testimonies of those who have been freed from depression are reminders that God is still at work and that no chain is too strong for Him to break.

Tearing Down Spiritual Strongholds

Depression not only affects our minds and emotions, but it can also be a spiritual stronghold in our lives. Strongholds are patterns of thought that rise up against the knowledge of God and keep us enslaved. However, God has given us powerful spiritual weapons to tear down these strongholds:

"The weapons we fight with are not the weapons of the world. On the contrary, they have divine power to demolish strongholds. We demolish arguments and every pretension that sets itself up against the knowledge of God, and we take captive every thought to make it obedient to Christ." — 2 Corinthians 10:4-5

To break the chains of depression, we must take control of our thoughts and bring them into obedience to Christ. This means not allowing negative and destructive thoughts to control our minds but replacing them with God's truth.

The Role of Faith and Perseverance

Breaking the chains of depression is not always an instant process. Sometimes, it can be a daily battle that requires faith and perseverance. God calls us to walk by faith and trust that, even when we don't see immediate results, He is working in our lives.

"For we live by faith, not by sight." — 2 Corinthians 5:7

Through faith, we can see beyond our current circumstances and hold onto God's promises.

Perseverance in prayer, praise, and meditating on His Word strengthens and equips us to keep moving forward, trusting that God will give us the victory.

Key Verse for This Chapter

Psalm 40:1-2 is a testimony of the deliverance God can bring into our lives when we cry out to Him:

> *"I waited patiently for the Lord; he turned to me and heard my cry. He lifted me out of the slimy pit, out of the mud and mire; he set my feet on a rock and gave me a firm place to stand."*

God not only hears our cry but lifts us out of the pit of despair and places us on solid ground. This verse is a reminder that, even though depression is deep, God's power is greater, and He can pull us out of any abyss.

Before concluding this chapter, I encourage you to say this prayer:

Father, You are the God who breaks chains. Today, I ask You to break the chains of depression that have held my heart and mind captive. I declare that in the name of Jesus, I am free. Renew my mind and my spirit, and let every lie of the enemy be replaced by the truth of Your Word. I ask You to guide me through this healing process and help me walk in the freedom You have promised me. Amen.

Chapter 5

The Power of Praise and Worship

Praise and worship are powerful spiritual tools that God has given us to combat sadness, discouragement, and depression. Through praise, we not only express our gratitude and love to God, but we also experience an inner transformation. Praise changes the spiritual atmosphere, releasing peace and joy, even in the darkest moments. In this chapter, we will explore how praise and worship can be a source of healing and strength in the midst of depression, and how we can integrate them into our daily lives to experience God's presence in a refreshing way.

How Praise Transforms the Atmosphere

The Bible is full of examples of how praise changes the atmosphere and brings victory. One of the most significant stories is that of King Jehoshaphat in *2 Chronicles 20*. Faced with an imminent threat from enemies coming to destroy Israel, Jehoshaphat sought God in prayer. God gave him an unusual strategy: to send the singers and musicians ahead of the army to praise the Lord. As they did this, something incredible happened—the enemies of Israel became confused and destroyed each other.

"As they began to sing and praise, the Lord set ambushes against the men of Ammon and Moab and Mount Seir who were invading Judah, and they were defeated." — 2 Chronicles 20:22

This story shows us that praise is not just an act of worship, but a spiritual weapon. When we praise God, we are declaring His greatness and power, and this changes the atmosphere around us. Even when we are struggling with depression, praise has the power to break the chains of oppression and open the door for God to work in our lives.

Praise as a Spiritual Weapon

When we are depressed, praising God may be the last thing we feel like doing. However, it is precisely in these moments that praise is most powerful. By choosing to worship God despite our emotions, we demonstrate our faith in His goodness and power. Praise shifts our focus: instead of dwelling on our problems, we focus on God, who is greater than any circumstance.

David, the psalmist, understood this very well. Throughout the Psalms, we see how David used praise as a way to lift his spirit in times of despair. A powerful example can be found in *Psalm 42:11:*

"Why, my soul, are you downcast? Why so disturbed within me? Put your hope in God, for I will yet praise Him, my Savior and my God."

David spoke to his own soul, reminding himself of the importance of praising God even in the midst of anguish. He knew that praise had the power to lift him from despair and restore his hope.

Biblical Examples of Praise in Times of Anguish

The Bible gives us many examples of people who faced great challenges and, through praise, found strength and deliverance. One of the most well-known stories is that of Paul and Silas in prison. After being unjustly arrested, beaten, and chained in a dark cell, Paul and Silas did something surprising: they began to pray and sing hymns of praise to God.

"About midnight Paul and Silas were praying and singing hymns to God, and the other prisoners were listening to them. Suddenly there was such a violent earthquake that the foundations of the prison were shaken. At once all the prison doors flew open, and everyone's chains came loose." — Acts 16:25-26

This passage teaches us that praise has the power to shake the foundations of any prison, whether literal or spiritual. The chains that held them were broken, and they were set free. Praise not only changed their physical situation but also their spiritual atmosphere. Although their circumstances did not change immediately, their spirits were lifted through praising God, which ultimately led to their deliverance.

Like Paul and Silas, when we praise God in the midst of our depression, the chains of sadness, discouragement, and despair can be broken. Praise releases God's power to work in our situation.

Practical Guide to Praise

Incorporating praise into our daily lives is not always easy, especially when we are struggling with depression. However, there are simple ways to start cultivating a life of praise, even in the midst of difficulties:

1. **Sing or listen to praise music**: Music has a powerful impact on our emotions. Listening to songs that exalt God's name can help redirect our focus towards Him and lift our spirits.
2. **Declare God's greatness**: Praising God is not just about singing but also about declaring who He is. Even when you don't feel well, you can proclaim: "God, You are good. You are faithful. I know You love me and have control."
3. **Praise in prayer**: Dedicate time to pray and thank God for His blessings. Even in the midst of depression, we can find reasons to be grateful: life, God's love, His grace, and mercy.
4. **Keep a praise journal**: Sometimes, writing our praises can be an effective way to express gratitude and focus on the positive. Keeping a journal where you note why you

praise God each day can change your perspective.

Praise Changes the Heart

Praise not only transforms the spiritual atmosphere but also changes our hearts. When we focus on God and His goodness, we experience an inner transformation. Depression tends to make us focus on ourselves and our circumstances, but praise redirects us towards God. As we do this, we begin to see our circumstances through the eyes of faith, knowing that God is in control and that, although the pain is real, He is greater than any storm we face.

"You will keep in perfect peace those whose minds are steadfast because they trust in You."
— *Isaiah 26:3*

This verse reminds us that when we keep our focus on God, He keeps us in peace. Praise is a way to persevere in our thoughts towards God, constantly reminding us that He is our peace and strength.

Key Verse for this Chapter

Psalm 42:11 is a powerful reminder that, even in the darkest moments, praising God can lift our spirits and restore our hope:

"Why, my soul, are you downcast? Why so disturbed within me? Put your hope in God, for I will yet praise Him, my Savior and my God."

This verse not only invites us to praise God in times of difficulty but also assures us that God is our salvation. By placing our hope in Him and praising Him, we find the strength we need to move forward.

Before concluding this chapter, I encourage you to pray this prayer:

God, teach me to praise You even when I don't feel like it. I know there is power in praise, and today I surrender my pain and my circumstances to You. May my praise be a spiritual weapon against depression, and may Your presence surround me when I lift my voice to glorify You. In the midst of the storm, may I find joy in worshiping You, knowing that You are worthy of all my praise, in every moment. In Jesus' name, amen.

Chapter 6

Restoring Life's Purpose with God

Depression can make us feel as if our lives have lost meaning, leaving us trapped in hopelessness. Many people who struggle with depression experience a deep disconnect from their sense of purpose, feeling as if they've lost their way or that they no longer have a meaningful destination in life. However, God's truth tells us otherwise. Each of us has a purpose designed by our Creator, and when we reconnect with that divine purpose, we find hope, direction, and a reason to live.

In this chapter, we will explore how depression affects our perception of purpose and how, with God's help, we can regain a clear vision of what He has planned for our lives.

God Has a Plan for Each of Us

From the very beginning of our lives, God has already established a plan for us. This doesn't mean we won't face challenges or difficult times, but it is essential to remember that, in the midst of it all, God has a purpose for each one of us. One of the most powerful verses that assures us of this truth is *Jeremiah 29:11:*

"For I know the plans I have for you," declares the Lord, "plans to prosper you and not to harm you, plans to give you hope and a future."

This verse reminds us that even though our current circumstances may be difficult, God's plan for our lives is full of hope and peace. He has a clear purpose for us, even when we can't see it for ourselves. Our task is to seek His will and trust His guidance, knowing that He will lead us to where we need to be.

When we are depressed, we may feel as if we've lost our way, but the good news is that God is always ready to guide us back to His purpose. He has never forgotten us, and His plan remains, waiting for us to return to Him to discover it.

Restoring Hope Through Purpose

One reason depression can feel so overwhelming is that it distorts our view of the future. The enemy works to convince us that there is no hope, that our efforts are pointless, and that our lives lack purpose. However, when we align ourselves with God's will, we regain hope. Our purpose is not based on our abilities or circumstances, but on what God has designed for us.

"And we know that in all things God works for the good of those who love Him, who have been called according to His purpose." — *Romans 8:28*

This verse assures us that, regardless of the circumstances we face, God is working for our good. He uses even the difficult situations to shape us and draw us closer to His purpose. This gives us hope, knowing that our suffering is not in vain. Through our faith in God, even moments of depression can be used to transform us and prepare us for what He has planned.

Discovering Your Calling in God

God's purpose for our lives is not always immediately clear, but His Word gives us the keys to discovering it. Here are some ways to begin seeking and uncovering your calling in God:

1. **Seek God in Prayer**: Prayer is a continuous conversation with God. As we spend time in His presence, He reveals His purpose for us. It is important to ask God to show us what He has prepared for our lives.
2. **Read and Meditate on the Bible**: The Bible is the living Word of God, and through it, we can find direction and wisdom. Many of us have discovered our calling by reading God's Word and feeling that certain passages speak directly to our situation.
3. **Serve Others**: Sometimes, we discover our purpose by serving others. Jesus taught us to love our neighbors and to serve with humility. As we serve, God may reveal the gifts and talents He has placed within us and how we can use them for His glory.
4. **Listen to Spiritual Mentors**: God has given us leaders and mentors in the faith to help us find our way. Seeking the counsel and

prayer of mature Christians can be a valuable way to discern the purpose God has for us.

Discovering our calling is not an instant process, but one that requires patience, faith, and a willingness to listen to God's voice. However, when we sincerely seek His will, He is faithful to show us the way.

Walking in God's Plans

Once we begin to discover God's purpose for our lives, we must commit to walking in that plan with faith and obedience. God not only reveals His purpose to us but also gives us the strength and tools we need to fulfill it. Walking in God's plans means trusting His guidance, even when we don't understand all the details or when the path seems difficult.

"Trust in the Lord with all your heart and lean not on your own understanding; in all your ways submit to Him, and He will make your paths straight." — Proverbs 3:5-6

This verse encourages us to trust God completely. Often, we try to control our lives and make decisions based on our own logic. But true success in God's purpose lies in trusting His guidance, knowing that He has a broader and perfect perspective of what we need.

Walking in God's plans also means being obedient to His calling, even when it's not easy. Obedience is a demonstration of our faith that His plan is better than anything we could imagine for ourselves.

God's Purpose Brings Life and Restoration

When we begin to walk in God's purpose, something incredible happens—we experience restoration and renewal. Depression tends to steal our life and joy, but when we find and follow God's purpose, we find life in abundance. Jesus promised that He came to give us life, and that life would be abundant:

"The thief comes only to steal and kill and destroy; I have come that they may have life, and have it to the full." — John 10:10

This verse is a declaration of the victory we have in Christ. The enemy wants to steal our purpose and destroy our peace, but Jesus offers us a full and meaningful life. When we follow His plan, we experience a life filled with joy, hope, and purpose.

The Role of Faith in Pursuing Purpose

Restoring life's purpose with God is not always a straightforward or easy process. Faith plays a crucial role in this journey. Depression may try to cloud our vision and convince us that we will never find our purpose, but it is in those moments that we must walk by faith and not by sight.

"For we walk by faith, not by sight." — 2 Corinthians 5:7

Walking by faith means trusting that God is working in our lives, even when we cannot see immediate results. It means believing that He has a plan, even when our current circumstances tell us otherwise. By keeping our faith firmly in God, we can move forward, knowing that His purpose for us will be revealed in His time.

Key Verse for This Chapter

Jeremiah 29:11 is a clear promise that God has a purpose and a future full of hope for each of us:

"For I know the plans I have for you," declares the Lord, "plans to prosper you and not to harm you, plans to give you hope and a future."

This verse should be an anchor for us in times of uncertainty. No matter what we are going through, God has a plan full of hope and life for us. By seeking His will and walking in His ways, we will find the purpose He has specifically designed for us.

Before concluding this chapter, I encourage you to pray this prayer:

Lord, many times I feel lost and without purpose, but I know that You have a plan for my life. I ask You to help me regain that sense of purpose that comes from You. Reveal Your ways to me, and may I walk in the direction You have prepared for my life. Help me to trust that You will guide me and that Your plan is perfect, even when I don't fully understand it. Thank You for creating me with a purpose. Amen.

Chapter 7

The Importance of the Christian Community

Depression can often make us feel isolated, alone in our struggle, and disconnected from the world around us. This isolation is not only emotional but also spiritual. However, God designed us to live in community, surrounded by other believers who support, encourage, and guide us in our walk with Christ. In times of depression, the Christian community is one of the greatest sources of strength and support that God has given us. This chapter explores the importance of the Christian community and how it can be a refuge for those who are struggling with depression.

The Power of Fellowship

The Bible teaches us that believers are not called to walk alone, but in fellowship with one another. From the beginning of creation, God declared that it is not good for man to be alone

(Genesis 2:18), reflecting His design for us to live in community. In the New Testament, the early church lived out this truth daily. The early Christians gathered regularly to pray, share, and support each other.

"And they devoted themselves to the apostles' teaching and the fellowship, to the breaking of bread and the prayers." – Acts 2:42

This verse shows how the early church understood the importance of fellowship and mutual support. In times of struggle, such as when we are dealing with depression, we need a community to hold us up. It's not just about attending church or gathering with other believers, but about living in intimate, genuine relationships with fellow Christians who can help us stay strong in faith.

Christian fellowship provides a safe place where we can be vulnerable and honest about our struggles. By sharing our burdens with other believers, we remind ourselves that we are not alone in our battle. Often, others have gone through similar situations and can offer comfort, prayers, and practical support.

The Church as a Body

The Bible describes the church as the "body of Christ," where each member has an important role and contributes to the well-being of the whole body. This concept, expressed in 1 Corinthians 12, is key to understanding the importance of the Christian community in times of weakness.

"For just as the body is one and has many members, and all the members of the body, though many, are one body, so it is with Christ."
– 1 Corinthians 12:12

Each of us is part of this body, and none of us are meant to function in isolation. When one member of the body suffers, the whole body suffers. Likewise, when one member is strengthened, the whole body is edified. This passage teaches us that we need each other and that others need us.

In times of depression, it can be easy to withdraw and isolate ourselves, but doing so only distances us from the vital support that the Christian community can provide. When we are surrounded by fellow believers who pray for us, encourage us, and lift us up in moments of weakness, we experience the power of the body of Christ in action.

The Importance of Sharing Our Burdens

One of the most important principles in the Christian community is sharing our burdens with one another. God has not called us to carry our struggles alone. Depression, in particular, is a heavy burden that we should not bear on our own. The Bible encourages us to share our difficulties with other believers so that we may be strengthened and supported.

"Bear one another's burdens, and so fulfill the law of Christ." – Galatians 6:2

This verse calls us to carry the problems and struggles of our brothers and sisters in faith. By doing so, we fulfill the law of Christ, which is love. In the Christian community, we not only find emotional support but also spiritual support. Our brothers and sisters in Christ can pray for us, intercede before God on our behalf, and offer words of encouragement based on the Word of God.

It's important to remember that sharing our burdens is not a sign of weakness, but of wisdom. Often, the enemy wants us to feel ashamed or believe that we must deal with our struggles on our own. But God has given us the community so that we are not alone in our difficulties.

How to Be a Supportive Friend

Just as it is important to receive support from the Christian community, we are also called to be a source of encouragement and support for others. In times of depression, it's easy to focus solely on our own struggles, but one way to find healing is by serving and supporting others who are also going through difficult times.

Jesus taught us to love our neighbor as ourselves (*Matthew 22:39*). This means being sensitive to the needs of others, paying attention to those who may be struggling in silence, and offering our help, whether through prayer, words of encouragement, or acts of service.

Some practical ways to be a supportive friend include:

1. **Listen without judgment**: Sometimes, people who are depressed just need someone to listen without offering immediate solutions. The simple presence of an understanding friend can be of great help.

2. **Pray for them**: Prayer is one of the most powerful ways to support someone. Pray regularly for those who are struggling with depression, asking God to give them peace, healing, and guidance.

3. **Encourage with God's Word**: Sharing Bible verses that speak of God's hope and comfort can bring relief and remind them that they are not alone.

4. **Offer practical help**: Sometimes, small things like helping with tasks, offering company, or simply being present can make a big difference in the life of someone who is depressed.

The Christian Community as a Refuge

In moments of greatest weakness, the Christian community acts as a refuge. God designed us to live in fellowship, and when we connect with other believers, we find a safe place where we can be vulnerable and receive the love of Christ through His body.

"God is our refuge and strength, a very present help in trouble." – Psalm 46:1

This verse reminds us that God is our refuge, and many times He uses His people, the church, to be a tangible manifestation of that refuge. The Christian community is not perfect, but when it is rooted in the love of Christ, it becomes a place where we can find strength in the most difficult times.

Key Verse for This Chapter

Ecclesiastes 4:9-10 highlights the importance of community and how God calls us to support each other:

"Two are better than one, because they have a good reward for their toil. For if they fall, one will lift up his fellow. But woe to him who is alone when he falls and has not another to lift him up!"

This verse illustrates the need to have someone to lift us when we fall. The Christian community is designed to be that support, to lift us when we are weak and in need.

In this chapter, we have seen how vital the Christian community is in our battle against depression. God has given us the church so that we do not walk alone but so that we support and strengthen each other in faith. As we seek healing and restoration in God, it is essential that we connect with a community of believers who can walk with us on this journey. Together, as the body of Christ, we can find the strength and encouragement needed to overcome any struggle we face.

Before concluding this chapter, I encourage you to pray this prayer:

Heavenly Father, I thank You for the Christian community You have given me. Help me to open my heart to the people You have placed in my path to support me. Give me the humility to ask for help when I need it, and teach me to be a good friend and brother to others. May my life be surrounded by people who encourage me in my faith, and together we may walk toward healing and growth in You. In Jesus' name, amen.

Chapter 8

Prayer and Spiritual Counseling to Overcome Depression

Depression is an emotional, mental, and spiritual battle that we often cannot face alone. God has given us powerful tools to combat this enemy, and two of the most effective are prayer and spiritual counseling. Prayer connects us with the heart of God, allowing us to cry out to Him in our pain and receive His peace and guidance. Spiritual counseling provides the support and direction we need to move forward, with the wisdom of those who are trained to guide us in our faith.

This chapter explores how prayer and spiritual counseling can help us overcome depression, providing a pathway to healing and restoration in God.

Prayer as the Foundation

Prayer is our direct connection with God. Through prayer, we have the opportunity to pour out our hearts before the Lord, tell Him our struggles, and receive His comfort and guidance. When we are depressed, prayer is not always easy. Sometimes the pain is so deep that we don't know what to say or how to start. But the Bible assures us that even in our darkest moments, God is listening.

"Call to me and I will answer you, and will tell you great and hidden things that you have not known." – Jeremiah 33:3

This verse is a promise that when we cry out to God, He hears us and answers us. Sometimes that answer comes in the form of peace, other times in guidance, but we can always trust that God is working in our favor, even when we cannot see it. Prayer, at its core, is an act of faith, a way to cast our burdens on God and trust that He has the power to lift us up.

Types of Prayer for Times of Depression

During depression, different types of prayer can help us connect with God and receive His healing. Here are some examples of prayers you can incorporate into your life:

1. **Prayer of Crying Out**: In moments of desperation, simply crying out to God is one of the most powerful prayers. You don't need elaborate words, just a sincere heart willing to seek His help. Crying out can be an expression of the pain you are feeling, but also an expression of faith that God is with you.

2. **Prayer of Gratitude**: Even in the midst of depression, gratitude can transform our hearts. By thanking God for the blessings we do have, we remember His goodness and faithfulness. Sometimes, making a list of things we are thankful for can help shift our perspective.

3. **Prayer of Intercession**: Although we may be struggling, praying for others allows us to step outside our own situation and focus on the well-being of others. This act of love and service can be a source of healing, reminding us that we are not alone in our battles.

4. **Prayer of Confession**: Sometimes depression may be linked to unhealed wounds or sins we have not confessed. Opening our hearts to God and asking Him to cleanse us of

all guilt and pain is crucial for our healing. *Psalm 51* is a great example of a prayer of confession, where David cries out to God for purification and restoration.

The Peace of God in Prayer

Prayer is not only a means of asking for help but also a way to receive the peace that only God can give. When we come to Him in prayer, we hand over our burdens, anxieties, and fears, and in exchange, we receive His peace.

"Do not be anxious about anything, but in everything by prayer and supplication with thanksgiving let your requests be made known to God. And the peace of God, which surpasses all understanding, will guard your hearts and your minds in Christ Jesus." – Philippians 4:6-7

This verse is a promise that when we bring our concerns to God, He gives us His peace—a peace that goes beyond our understanding. It doesn't mean all our problems will disappear immediately, but it does mean we can face our struggles with an inner calm that comes from trusting in God.

The Role of Spiritual Counseling

Spiritual counseling is an essential ministry within the body of Christ and can be a great help for those struggling with depression. Through counseling, we receive the wisdom and support of Christian leaders who have been called and trained to guide us according to God's Word. It is not just emotional therapy but guidance based on biblical principles that can help us find clarity and purpose in the midst of confusion.

"Where there is no guidance, a people falls, but in an abundance of counselors there is safety." – Proverbs 11:14

This verse highlights the importance of seeking counsel. In times of struggle, it's easy to fall into the trap of trying to carry the burden alone. However, God has placed spiritual counselors in our path to help us see things from a biblical perspective and find solutions that align with His will.

How to Find the Right Spiritual Counselor

Not all spiritual counselors are the same, and it is important to seek someone who is firmly rooted in the Word of God and sensitive to the leading of the Holy Spirit. Here are some steps to find the right counselor:

1. **Pray for direction**: Ask God to guide you to the right person, someone with the discernment needed to help you in your healing process.
2. **Look for a mature leader in the faith**: Ideally, find someone with ministry experience and a solid testimony of faith. A pastor, church elder, or certified Christian counselor can be a good option.
3. **Trust the process**: Spiritual counseling doesn't always bring immediate answers, but it is a process that will help you grow and find healing. Be honest and open in your conversations, trusting that God is using this person to guide you.

The Importance of Prayer and Counseling Together

Prayer and spiritual counseling are not separate options but should go hand in hand. As you pray and seek God's guidance in your life, counseling can help you understand what God is revealing, providing you with practical and spiritual support to overcome depression.

Prayer is your direct connection with God, and counseling is a resource God offers you through His church. By using both, you can be sure that you are walking on the path of healing that God has designed for you.

Key Verse for This Chapter

Philippians 4:6-7 is a powerful reminder that prayer is the key to receiving God's peace in any situation:

"Do not be anxious about anything, but in everything by prayer and supplication with thanksgiving let your requests be made known to God. And the peace of God, which surpasses all understanding, will guard your

hearts and your minds in Christ Jesus."
This verse assures us that God's peace will guard our hearts and minds when we bring our burdens to Him in prayer. It's a promise that even in the midst of depression, prayer is the channel through which we receive God's peace and strength.

In this chapter, we have explored how prayer and spiritual counseling are essential tools for overcoming depression. Through prayer, we can connect our hearts with God, find peace, and surrender our struggles to Him. Through spiritual counseling, we find the support and direction we need to walk toward healing. God has provided both tools for our restoration, and by using them together, we can move forward toward freedom in Christ.

Before concluding this chapter, I encourage you to pray this prayer:

God, today I come to You in prayer, knowing that You hear me and that I find comfort in You. Help me to be consistent in my prayer and to seek You daily. I ask that You guide me to spiritual counselors who can help me in this healing process. May I hear Your voice through them and may they help me walk closer to You. Give me the peace that surpasses all understanding and the wisdom to move forward with faith. Amen.

Chapter 9

Maintaining Peace and Joy in God

Depression is an intense battle that can wear down both the soul and the body, but with God's help, it is possible to find peace and joy, even in the midst of difficulties. Once we have begun the healing process, the next step is to learn how to maintain the peace and joy that God gives us. This chapter will focus on how to sustain peace and joy in God by cultivating a life of prayer, worship, trust in His promises, and walking with a mindset renewed by His Word.

The Peace That Surpasses All Understanding

God's peace is not like the peace the world offers. The peace that comes from God does not depend on our circumstances but on His constant presence in our lives. Jesus Himself promised us this peace in the midst of any storm.

"Peace I leave with you; my peace I give you. I do not give to you as the world gives. Do not let your hearts be troubled, and do not be afraid."
– John 14:27

When we face depression, our emotions and thoughts can be in chaos. However, Jesus' promise is that we can have peace, even when everything around us seems out of control. This peace is not based on what we feel but on the certainty that God is with us, walking beside us.

The key to maintaining this peace is to keep our focus on God. In *Isaiah 26:3*, we are promised:

"You will keep in perfect peace those whose minds are steadfast because they trust in you."

Keeping our thoughts focused on God means remembering His promises, trusting in His faithfulness, and not letting the circumstances of life divert us from that trust. God's peace is a gift, but we must be intentional in keeping our minds focused on Him.

Joy as the Fruit of the Spirit

Joy in God is a gift that goes beyond temporary emotions. It's not just about being happy or feeling good but about a deep inner joy that comes from a relationship with God. This joy is the fruit of the Holy Spirit, who dwells in us as believers.

"But the fruit of the Spirit is love, joy, peace, forbearance, kindness, goodness, faithfulness, gentleness, and self-control." – Galatians 5:22-23

Joy is something the Spirit produces in us when we live in communion with God. It's a joy that does not depend on external circumstances but on the certainty that God is working in our lives for our good. Even in the midst of trials, we can experience that deep joy.

To maintain this joy, it is essential to remain in God's presence. David, the psalmist, understood this when he wrote:

"You make known to me the path of life; you will fill me with joy in your presence, with

eternal pleasures at your right hand." – Psalm 16:11

Being in God's presence—whether in prayer, worship, or meditation on His Word—fills us with joy. When our lives are centered on Him, we find a joy that the world cannot take away.

Staying in God's Word

One of the most effective ways to maintain peace and joy is to live in God's Word. Scripture is our guide for understanding who God is and how we should live. The Bible gives us God's promises that we can remember in times of difficulty, and by meditating on it, our minds are renewed.

"Blessed is the one who does not walk in step with the wicked or stand in the way that sinners take or sit in the company of mockers, but whose delight is in the law of the Lord, and who meditates on his law day and night. That person is like a tree planted by streams of water, which yields its fruit in season and whose leaf does not wither—whatever they do prospers." – Psalm 1:1-3

This passage shows that when our lives are rooted in God's Word, we are like trees planted by streams of water—strong and fruitful. God's Word sustains us, nourishes us, and keeps us firm, even in the midst of life's storms.

Trusting in God's Promises

God has given us many promises in His Word, and trusting in them is key to maintaining peace and joy. When we trust what God has promised, we can rest in the certainty that He will fulfill His words.

"The one who calls you is faithful, and he will do it." – 1 Thessalonians 5:24

God is faithful. We can trust that He will do everything He has promised. Although our feelings may fluctuate, God's faithfulness is constant. Trusting in His promises gives us a solid foundation upon which to build our lives.

Constant Prayer as a Source of Peace and Joy

Prayer is not just a moment of communication with God but a way of life that allows us to remain in His peace and joy. Constant prayer helps us keep our minds focused on Him, bring our concerns to His feet, and receive His comfort.

"Pray continually. Give thanks in all circumstances, for this is God's will for you in Christ Jesus." – 1 Thessalonians 5:17-18

The call to pray continually doesn't mean being in a constant physical posture of prayer but rather maintaining an attitude of continual prayer, a continuous connection with God in every situation. Through prayer, we cast our burdens, receive direction, and are strengthened to face any circumstance.

Worship as a Lifestyle

Worship is not just about singing songs on Sundays; it's a lifestyle that places God at the center of everything we do. When we live a life of worship, recognizing God's greatness in every aspect of our lives, our circumstances begin to lose their power over us. Worship helps us focus on who God is, not on what we are going through.

"Yet a time is coming and has now come when the true worshipers will worship the Father in the Spirit and in truth, for they are the kind of worshipers the Father seeks." – John 4:23

By living in worship, we acknowledge God as sovereign in our lives, and that fills us with peace and joy because we know He is in control.

Walking with a Renewed Mind

One of the greatest challenges to maintaining peace and joy in God is the battle in our minds. Depression can fill us with negative thoughts, but God's Word teaches us that we must renew our minds with His truth.

"Do not conform to the pattern of this world, but be transformed by the renewing of your mind. Then you will be able to test and approve what God's will is—His good, pleasing, and perfect will." – Romans 12:2

Renewing our minds is a daily process that involves rejecting destructive thoughts and replacing them with God's truth. By meditating on Scripture and allowing the Holy Spirit to transform our way of thinking, we begin to see life from God's perspective, which brings us peace and joy.

Key Verse for This Chapter

Isaiah 26:3 reminds us of God's promise to keep us in peace if we keep our minds focused on Him:

"You will keep in perfect peace those whose minds are steadfast because they trust in you."

This verse is a powerful truth that encourages us to persevere in our thoughts toward God. By trusting Him and focusing on His truth, we experience a peace that cannot be taken away by circumstances.

In this chapter, we have explored how to maintain peace and joy in God through prayer, meditation on His Word, trust in His promises, and the renewal of our minds. Although struggles may continue, God offers us a peace and joy that surpass all understanding if we remain in His presence and walk with a mind renewed by His truth.

Before concluding this chapter, I encourage you to say this prayer:

Lord, give me the peace and joy that only You can give. Help me to keep my mind fixed on You so that I am not shaken by the circumstances of life. Teach me to trust in Your promises and to live in the fullness of joy that You offer. Through prayer and worship, may my heart be filled with peace, and may Your joy be my strength every day. In Jesus' name, Amen.

Chapter 10

Testimonies and Conclusion: Walking in Faith Toward the Future

Throughout this book, we have explored the journey of depression, the process of healing with God's help, and how prayer, praise, Christian community, and trusting in God's promises are key to finding and maintaining peace and joy. One of the most powerful ways to see God's power in action is through the testimonies of people who, like you, have struggled with depression and have experienced God's restoration and purpose in their lives.

This final chapter will focus on sharing testimonies of people who have overcome depression with God's help, while also giving you a final word of encouragement to walk toward the future in faith, knowing that God is with you every step of the way.

Testimonies of Healing Through God

Testimonies are more than just stories; they are living proof of God's transformative power. Here are a few testimonies from young people who have found freedom from depression through their faith in God.

Testimony 1: Sara – From Darkness to Light

Sara was a young woman who struggled with deep depression from her teenage years. She felt like she didn't fit in, believed she had no value, and thought her life had no meaning. Although she grew up in a Christian family, her relationship with God grew cold as her depression deepened. At one point, she even considered ending her life.

One day, a friend invited her to a youth group at her church. At first, Sara went out of courtesy, but little by little, she began to feel something different. During a night of prayer, she decided to open her heart to God. That night, she prayed sincerely, asking God to help her climb out of the pit she was in.

"I realized that I had been struggling alone for a long time. I felt a peace I had never experienced before, and since that day, God has been restoring my life. It hasn't been easy, but now I know I'm not alone. I've found a purpose in Him, and with each passing day, I trust more in His plan."

Sara still faces challenges, but her relationship with God has sustained her. Now, she helps other young people who are dealing with similar problems, sharing her testimony of how God brought her out of the darkness.

Testimony 2: Luis – The Power of Prayer and the Christian Community

Luis had always been active in his church, but when his father died unexpectedly, depression consumed him. He lost interest in life, and although he continued attending church, he felt empty inside. For months, he struggled in silence, without telling anyone what he was going through. It was a time when he felt completely disconnected from God.

One day, his pastor called him and asked how he was doing. After much persistence, Luis finally confessed what he had been feeling. His pastor and several church members began praying for him, and Luis also decided to seek Christian counseling.

"I felt like I had been carrying a weight that wouldn't let me breathe, but prayer and my church community began to lift me. It wasn't immediate, but as I opened up more to God and my community, I began to feel renewed."

Luis is now stronger in his faith than ever, grateful for the support he received and for God's restoring power. Through prayer, counseling, and the support of his Christian community, he found a new reason to live.

Testimony 3: Carla – Praise as a Weapon Against Depression

Carla had been struggling with depression since her teenage years. She felt overwhelmed by the expectations of others, and the pressure from social media and school only worsened her emotional state. Although she attended church, she didn't feel she had a close relationship with God.

Everything changed during a worship retreat at her church. During a time of worship, she felt a deep release as she sang. In that moment, something changed in her heart.

"Praise was like a key that opened a door inside me. I felt like the Holy Spirit was there, healing wounds I had carried for years. Since then, whenever I feel depressed, I lift my voice in praise, and God's peace surrounds me."

Carla discovered that praise is not only an act of worship but also a form of spiritual warfare. Now, instead of letting depression drag her down, she uses praise to draw closer to God and remember His faithfulness.

Testimony 4: Ana – Peace at 45 Years Old

Ana had been battling depression for several years. After going through a divorce and financial problems, she began to feel that her life was out of control. The sadness overwhelmed her, and she often felt alone, even when surrounded by people.

"There were days when I simply didn't have the strength to get out of bed. I felt like I had failed at everything: my family, my career, and my relationship with God. I couldn't understand why this was happening to me."

One day, while browsing the internet, I found a Christian video by Pastor David Rodriguez Inca about the power of prayer. This motivated me to try once again to draw closer to God.

"I decided to start praying again, although at first, I didn't know what to say. Slowly, prayer became my refuge. I felt like God was lifting my burdens. I started reading the Bible again, and I clung to verses like Philippians 4:6-7, which reminded me that I could bring all my worries to God."

Over time, Ana's depression began to lift. Although it wasn't an instant change, she started to feel stronger emotionally and spiritually. Today, Ana continues to face challenges, but now she knows she is not alone.

"God has shown me that even in the darkest moments, He is present. Now, I live in peace, knowing that my life is in His hands."

Testimony 5: Manuel – A New Hope in God at 62 Years Old

Manuel is a 62-year-old man who, after a life of hard work and many responsibilities, found himself trapped in deep depression. He had gone through several personal losses: the death of his wife, retirement, and the estrangement of some of his children. All of this led him into an emotional loneliness he had never experienced before.

"I felt like my life no longer had meaning. I saw no reason to keep going and sank into a pit of sadness that seemed endless. The things that used to bring me joy no longer mattered, and I spent entire days without leaving the house. I felt completely disconnected from life, my family, and, most sadly, from God."

Although Manuel had been a man of faith his whole life, this period made him doubt God's closeness. He withdrew from church and stopped praying. However, one day, while talking to an old friend, he decided to attend a prayer group at his local church. At first, he went more out of obligation than desire, but something changed.

"One night, during a prayer meeting, I completely broke down. I cried like I hadn't in years. I asked God to help me, to bring me out of the darkness I was in. It was at that moment that I felt something I hadn't felt in a long time: a peace that didn't come from me but from God."

From that day forward, Manuel began to regain hope. Little by little, he started praying again and reading the Bible, something he had stopped doing. He found comfort in verses like *Isaiah 41:10*, which reminded him that God was with him, even in the darkest moments.

"It wasn't an immediate process, but day by day, I began to feel that God was restoring my life. The church community was key for me; the support of my friends and brothers in Christ upheld me in the most difficult moments. God showed me that He still had a purpose for me, that my life wasn't over, and that at any age, He can bring healing."

Today, Manuel dedicates his time to serving in his church, helping others who, like him, have gone through depression. He has learned that it's never too late to find peace and hope in God.

"If I could say one thing to people going through what I went through, it's that you are not alone. No matter how old you are, God has a plan for your life. With Him, there is always hope, and there is always a new opportunity to live with purpose."

Walking in Faith Toward the Future

The testimonies we've just read are proof that God can restore even the most broken areas of our lives. While each story is unique, they all share a common theme: God's faithfulness in bringing His children out of darkness and into the light.

As you move forward in your own journey toward healing, I want to remind you that this is a process. Healing doesn't always happen instantly, and there will be moments when you feel like you're stepping backward. But in those moments, it's when you need to cling to God the most, trusting that He will not abandon you.

"May God Himself, the God of peace, sanctify you through and through. May your whole spirit, soul, and body be kept blameless at the coming of our Lord Jesus Christ. The one who calls you is faithful, and He will do it." – 1 Thessalonians 5:23-24

This verse is a reminder that God is faithful, and if He has begun a work in you, He will complete it. Your story isn't over; God is writing every chapter of your life, and the best is yet to come.

The Power of Walking in Faith

Walking in faith means trusting in God even when we can't see the final result. It means believing that although depression may raise its head from time to time, God is greater and more powerful than any darkness. He has called you to a life of freedom, peace, and purpose, and His faithfulness will sustain you.

"For we live by faith, not by sight." – 2 Corinthians 5:7

This verse sums up how we should walk in our relationship with God. Even though we can't always see what God is doing behind the scenes, we can trust that He is working for our good. Faith drives us to keep moving forward, to keep trusting, and to keep seeking God, knowing that He is in control.

Final Words of Encouragement

As we conclude this book, I want to remind you that God will never abandon you. He is with you in every moment of your struggle, and His power is enough to lift you out of depression and bring you into a full life in His presence. As you walk into the future, do so with the confidence that God is guiding, restoring, and strengthening you every day.

"The Lord bless you and keep you; the Lord make His face shine on you and be gracious to you; the Lord turn His face toward you and give you peace." – Numbers 6:24-26

May God's peace accompany you in every step you take, and may His joy fill your heart as you trust in His perfect plan for your life.

With this chapter, we finish our journey through pain and into restoration with God. Although depression can be a difficult struggle, we are never alone. God walks beside us, offering His love, His peace, and His hope. May you continue moving forward in faith, knowing that the future God has planned for you is full of purpose, joy, and victory in Christ.

You are brave because you've come this far. Now, say this prayer—but don't let it be your last. From now on, keep praying and seeking more of God's fullness and the Holy Spirit.

Prayer:

Father, as I walk toward the future, I ask that You increase my faith. May the testimonies of Your faithfulness in the lives of others remind me that You are also working in my life. Help me trust that the best is yet to come and that You will guide me every step of the way. May my life be a living testimony of Your power and grace, and may I always walk in hope in You. Amen.

These prayers are designed to help you reflect on each topic, drawing you closer to God as you move forward in your process of healing and spiritual growth. May each prayer be an invitation to experience more of His love, His peace, and His power in your life.

Congratulations on making it this far! You're just one step away from completing this transformative journey. Each page has been a reminder that, with God's help, there is no darkness that can't be illuminated and no battle that can't be won. This is only the beginning of a new chapter in your life. Keep moving forward with faith, knowing that God is with you every step of the way. The best chapter is yet to be written in your life!

Conclusion

Throughout this book, we have walked a challenging but hope-filled path, exploring the reality of depression and how, with God's help, it is possible to overcome it. Depression is a very real battle, but it's a battle you don't have to face alone. In His love and mercy, God offers you His hand to lift you up, His peace to calm your mind, and His joy to fill your heart, even in the darkest moments.

We have seen how prayer, praise, the Christian community, spiritual counseling, and the power of God's Word are essential tools for finding healing and restoration. Though this path can be long and full of ups and downs, you are never without the company and comfort of your Heavenly Father. He is the one who heals broken hearts and strengthens those who feel overwhelmed.

It is important to remember that the healing process may not be immediate, but that doesn't mean God isn't working. Sometimes,

God's greatest work happens in the quietest and hardest moments of our lives. He is transforming your heart, renewing your mind, and preparing a future full of purpose and hope for you. No matter how deep the pit you find yourself in, God's grace is even deeper.

If there is one thing you should take from this book, it is that depression does not have the final word in your life. God has a purpose for you, and He is faithful to fulfill it. Every tear, every prayer, every moment of anguish is known to Him, and He is using it all for your good. Walk in faith toward what lies ahead, knowing that God's light illuminates each step you take, and in His love, you will find the strength you need to move forward.

May this book have been a beacon of hope for you, reminding you that even when storms come, you can always find refuge in God. As you continue your journey, trust that His peace, His joy, and His love will always accompany you.

May the God of all hope fill your heart with peace, and may you find in Him the fullness and purpose you long for. Move forward in faith and confidence, because your future is in the hands of the One who loves you without measure.

Made in the USA
Middletown, DE
26 November 2024